TODD MOORE

THE RIDDLE OF THE WOODEN GUN

ISBN 978-1-929878-01-7

First Printing
Published by LUMMOX Press
POB 5301
San Pedro, CA 90733

www.lummoxpress.com

Back cover photo by Pete Jonsson

Printed by CreateSpace.com

"Todd Moore runs with language and makes every word count."

--Elmore Leonard

"Violent, raw and riddled with humor, in time, Todd Moore's .44 magnum opus *Dillinger* will take its place in the American literary canon as one of the greatest. A longtime small press hero, Moore's gunshot stacca-to cannot be rivaled, there simply is no other. Literary outlaw and maverick poet, Todd Moore is a leader of the new romantic, a visionary wordslinger cut from the same bloody cloth as Cormac McCarthy."

--S.A. Griffin

"Todd Moore slaps you in the face and kicks your ass, with ink & paper."

--Joe Pachinko

"Bis vor kurzem hatte ich weder was von/ueber Todd Moore gehoert, geschweige denn gelesen. Beim Anhoeren einiger Zerx Kompilationen auf denen Todd hoechstpersoenlich seine Gedichte vortraegt, stellte sich bei mir dann das ein, was Todd in etwas so beschreibt: "Wenn's Deinen Arsch in Bewegung bringen soll, dann ein Gedicht". Alles was mir seitdem von Todd in die Finger kam wurde gelesen und gehoert und ich kann einfach nicht genug davon bekommen und seitdem kann ich auch wieder Blut sehen ohne gleich in Ohnmacht zu fallen."

--Klaus Thiemann., metropolis

"Moore is the real deal. What you see is exactly what you get. There's no fakery in his poetry. It's all meat, no filler."

--John Yamrus

THE RIDDLE

OF THE WOODEN GUN

WOOD all gone lost
half of the
known indi
viduals pres
ent at the
crown point
escape say
dillinger had
a real gun
the other
half state
he was in
possession
of a wooden
gun thus the
regional agent
in charge of
the investigation
cd not defini
tively offer
an opinion
four days
after dillin
ger's escape
he bought a
wooden gun
tie tack from
a novelty
shop in
chicago the
pistol itself
was a 45
automatic
a small pin
pierced the

barrel & the
point was
capped w/a
miniature
bullet that
held the
wooden
gun firmly
in place
dillinger
liked it so
much he
bought
billie one
her reaction
was i'd
rather have
a real one
wooden gun
stories i
got a million
of em
which one
wd you like
to hear
the old
man sd
blowing
the sha
vings off
the barrel
of the
wooden gun
he'd just
carved

then
handing
it across
to dillinger
who took
it smiled
& sd
tell me
one the
old man
clicked
his jack
knife shut
closed
his eyes
& sd
i used to
ride w/a
guerilla
outfit the
other side
of the
big river
coming
on dark
& we
were looking
for a good
place to
camp i
had this
feeling
the kind
i used to
get when

i cd tell
something
was gonna
happen
but i
didn't
know what
word had
been passed
along to
look out
for bush
whackers
my horse
was terrible
skittish &
a shadow
near a big
oak tree made
him rear
up a little
& when
he finally
settled down
i drew my
pistol i
was car
rying an
old walker
colt the
one my
daddy
carried down
in mexico
& when

that sha
dow moved
again i
fired that
damned old
44 used to
buck &
shake the
bones some
thing awful
& then i
heard some
thing fall
back into the
underbrush
& sticks
& such
so i dis
mount
real careful
& lead my
horse over
one or two
of the men
riding beside
me came
along too
i expected
to see some
hardbitten
old ridge
runner hol
ding a rifle
instead
it was a

kid & you
know what
alls he had
was a woo
den pistol
that's all
goddam his
fucked up
soul &
there he is
sprawled out
w/my 44
slug thru
his scrawny
chest eyes
all rolled back
like death
was the
best surprise
he cd ever
hope for
then what
dillinger asked
capn rode up
sd what's
the commotion
i pointed
to the kid
i'd shot &
the capn
shrugged
sd yankee
or if not
then who
knows let

the wolves
have him
i never sd
nothing but
i was
thinking
that the
wolves
already
had him
dillinger
shoved the
wooden gun
inside
his coat
& brought
out a snub
38 he held
it out butt
first & the
old man
wrapped
his bony
hand around
the grip
the whole
time trying
to be careful
not to put
his index
finger in
side the
trigger
guard he
glanced up

at dillinger
smiled
& sd it
feels light
then added
but then
death don't
weigh hardly
anything
just nothing
at all lost
wooden gun
tag was
the exact
opposite
of regular
tag van
meter sd
you had to
capture the
kid who
held the
wooden gun
see the
game worked
this way
you had
to pick the
longest straw
before you
cd have
the wooden
gun &
then you
had to be

fast enough
& tough
enough to
hold onto
it some
kids were
so tough
you cd
never get
the gun
away from
them ex
cept maybe
if they fell
down dropped
the gun &
you were
quick enough
to pick it up
& take off
w/it gun tag
was the toughest
tag i knew of
real desperado
stuff it involved
fists
feet
muscles
&
guts
you cd use
almost anything
as a wooden
gun but most
of us

just broke
sticks off
tree limbs
but it had
to be a stick
that had
another one
growing out
of it so that
it looked
as tho it had
a handle
& when
you got
called home
& you
were still
holding onto
that wooden
gun
hell
you broke
it in two
that meant
you won it
all
what was
it you won
dillinger asked
nothing
everything
mostly
the night
belongs to you
on his

way out
of millie's
diner dill
inger grabbed
a book of
matches
out of a bowl
sitting at
the end of
the counter
the book
cover was
a wooden
gun that read
dillinger's
escape gun
the counter
man sd take
a handful
& give one
to dillinger
for me
dillinger
grinned
& sd
don't mind
if i do
whenever the
federales
caught a
bandito in
mexico
they made
them dig
their own

graves
allowed them
to smoke
one last
cigaret
say a prayer
& then
they'd shoot
them in
the head
one clean
shot back
in the hair
then
& this was
a ritual
they'd nail
a wooden
gun to the
bandito's chest
as a warning
to others
mostly
tho
it was
a broken
off stick from
a rotting fence
how do you
know all
this dillinger
asked
the man
studied his
roll yr own

cigaret
smiled &
sd i used
to be a
member of
the federales
before the
revolution
& now
dillinger asked
the man
paused again
sd i'm
mostly
freelance
these days
dillinger
shoved some
thing in
to sam
cahoon's
back
cahoon
belched &
dillinger
sd if you
fart so
help me
i'll shoot
you in
the ass
dillinger had
heard of
the famed
wooden

pistols that
al capone
used to
award his
best pis
toleros for
jobs well
done
what made
those
wooden
guns so
rare was
the escutch
eon plates of
gold inlaid
in the grips
along w/
twenty dol
lar gold
pieces
also the
lucky shoo
ter's name
was en
graved in
the yellow
metal of
the escutch
eon plates
sometimes
mother of
pearl was
included
as an extra

incentive
while makley
was working
on a roll
yr own he
sd hey
johnnie
i'll bet
you never
heard this
one a
traveling
salesman
was having
coffee at
a little diner
he calls
the waitress
over & sez
see that
bulge in
my pocket
bet you can't
guess what
it is the
waitress
sez is it the
place where
yr so happy
to see me
the salesman
sez normally
it is
but today
it's where

i am carrying
my wooden
gun
wd you
like to touch
it waitress
sez you
ain't got
cooties
have you
the salesman
hauls the
wooden gun
out of his
pants pocket
& puts it
on the table
then sez
it's one a
my samples
i sell toy
guns then
as an after
thought he
sez now
wd you like
to see my
other one
the waitress
smiles sez
you can keep
yr wood
honey i'm
strictly a
meat kinda

girl
baby face
sd when i
was a kid
i used to
have a
wooden
gun but i
hammered
the grip
full of
bent nails
& broken
glass dill
inger sd
wasn't it
hard to
hold on
to w/out
cutting yr
self baby
face smiled
the essen
tial darkness
of his al
most very
white skin
sd i wore
a glove
only used
it to beat
the shit
outta kids
& that
wooden gun

worked
real nice
too
i put a
nail hole
in a kid's
cheek that
he's probably
still eating
apple pie
thru
questioned
as to visits
paid to
dillinger
while he
was in
carcerated
at crown point
which cul
minated in
a decision
not to have
the bureau
involved any
further in
such a
volatile
matter
not in those
words
but to that
effect
dillinger
hit one

unidentified
guard w/
the thompson
barrel so
hard that
one of his
teeth came
out &
bounced
down the
floor lost gone
i know a
guy piquette
sd
or at least
i used to
know him
anyway
he collected
guns
colt patersons
he told me
he saw
the original
wooden
pistol that
samuel
colt himself
had whittled
while he
was a sailor
& out
at sea
got the idea
for a revolver

from a ship's
wheel
no shit
it's true
so help me
god
where'd this
gun collector
see
samuel colt's
wooden gun
dillinger asked
jesus christ
you hadda
ask it was
out east
somewhere
lets see
gimme a
sec ok ok
it was the
wadsworth
something
& some
thing the
wadsworth
ath
eneum
of art out
in hartford
try saying
that 3 times
in a row
dillinger put
a 45 auto

out on the
table be
cause he
knew that
it wd irri
tate piquette
all to hell
now why
the fuck
wd you do
that piquette
asked
it needed
the air
dillinger sd
what kinda
horseshit
story is that
the same
kind as you
just got
done telling
christ i was
telling the
truth ok
maybe you
were des
cribe the
wooden gun
if you got
such a goddam
good memory
ok ok
piquette sd
this guy

& this sticks
in my mind
i don't know
why don't
ask me but
this guy sd
the first colt
revolver was
completely
carved from
wood but
the funny
thing is all
it was
was a
cylinder
a hammer
& a cyl
inder pin
parts
dillinger sd
pretending
to be
pissed off
he used
the auto
matic to
scratch an
itch in his
armpit
then he got
a slow smile
on his face
& sd
why in the

hell wd
the inventor
of the first
real
american
revolver
just carve
the cylinder
the hammer
& the goddam
cylinder pin
why wdn't
he do it all
up right
& carve out
the grip
the barrel
you gotta have
a barrel to
shoot thru
& the grip
you gotta have
a handle
to hold onto
if
you wanna
shoot the gun
see lou
ok
you get me
you know
that that's
how i can
tell that
you really

are fulla shit
johnny
johnny
when it
comes to
guns you
gotta be
lieve me
one thing
lou
yeah
what is it
how come
you know
so much
abt guns
but you
don't like
having any
around
dillinger
asked
pushing the
45 auto
against
piquette's
hand
piquette
smiled &
sd w/me
it's all
history &
dreams
i never
cared much

for the
shooting
part
come on
lou
if you care
abt history
then
you have
to know
it's all
abt shooting
the depart
ment is
actively see
king to ob
tain a trans
cript of tes
timony re
lating to
the piquette
case pen
ding any
further in
quiries
baby face
broke a
stick in
half then
sd i knew
this guy
on the west
coast who
used a woo
den gun as

his signature
whenever
he killed
someone
he'd shove
a wooden
gun under
the fucker's
head like
it was a
pillow
you know
sweet dreams
motherfucker
shit like that
was just
a little
reminder
abt who
was dish
ing out
death in
that part
of the
country
billie sd
hurry up
& stick it
in me
but be
goddam
careful
i don't
wanna be
getting

any splin
ters in
my cunt
or else
or else
what dill
inger sd
billie smiled
sd what
ever you
get in me
you get
in you
carried a
small woo
den gun
on a chain
around his
neck for
year as
a good
luck charm
wore it
right along
w/the cross
that bugs
moran
gave him
but it was
missing when
he was
found shot
dead in
a boone
county ditch

j edgar hoover
stood well
back while
his assistant
opened the
package
the assistant
shook the
big envelope
a couple of
times
& sd
no parts
moving
& it feels
pretty light
he took
his jack
knife out
clicked
the blade
open &
slit the
top all
the way
across
then he
pulled out
what first
appeared
to be a
38 special
but on
closer in
spection

realized
what it
was sd
well
i'll be
damned
what is it
hoover asked
moving
closer it's
a wooden
gun & hand
carved at
that wait
there's a
note that
came w/it
hoover
grabbed the
note out
of the
assistant's
hand &
read it
what's it
say the
assistant
asked hoo
ver handed
it over
& stood
staring into
space
mister hoover
the assistant

began
this is a
little memento
from crown
point i
thought
you'd like
to have
each &
every time
you birds
put me
away
i'll just
carve a
new one
i tried to
make this
one a
little
longer
than yr
dick
signed
john dillinger
wait
there's
a p.s.
this piece
of wood
might just
fit up yr
ass if
you treat
it real

nice
hoover
glanced
over at
hoover
whose face
had gone
white
he sd
the son
of a bitch
waddya
want me
to do
w/this
thing
the assistant
grabbed
the wooden
gun &
quickly
stuck it in
side his
suit coat
sd i'd
love to
burn the
goddam thing
but instead
it's going
into my
private
collection
then
as an after

thought
hoover sd
i want his
scalp
he slammed
his fist
down on
the desk
scattering
some papers
goddamit
i want his
scalp
somebody
had better
bring it back
to me
w/all the
hair still
on it
do you
want me
to issue a
memo to
that effect
no
jesus christ
no
we have
to show
some
discretion
but i'll have
that hair gone
dillinger

leaned acros
the bar
sd one eye
you run
a damn
fine speak
& you
never ask
questions
i like that
one eye sd
i'm gonna
break that
rule
how come
you only
drink coffee
or an
occasional
beer dill
inger blew
the head off
the brew that
one eye
had just
drawn sd
i gotta stay
clear
if i wanna
keep
breathing
now i got
a question
what's this
i hear abt

you giving
pancho villa
a solid gold
pistol
one eye
slapped a
bar rag over
his shoul
der &
laughed
sd you
ever notice
how a story
can grow
faster than
the size
of yr dick
when it's
glistening all
over w/cum &
w/cunt hair
ok dillinger
replied
then
tell me
the real
story
i used to
fly for villa
yeah i was
his air force
for awhile
i built the
goddam plane
in a texas

barn where
my old man
used to work
on cars
in fact for
awhile he
built his
own cars
& i built
my own
planes christ
it was nice
they were
based on
the curtis
pusher 30
caliber ma
chine gun
sat right in
front of me
the guy who
installed it
had it co
ordinated to
fire right
thru the
propelller
blade you
talk abt one
fucken smooth
piece of work
when guns
like that
talk all
death can

do is
shut the
fuck up
& listen
anyway
i knew
villa liked
getting
fancy pres
entation pis
tols you
know the
kind that
were en
graved w/
gold &
silver so
on the sly
i had one
ordered from
the colt
company &
it was
supposed
to arrive
on such &
such a date
naturally
villa didn't
know it
was coming
it was a
goddam sur
prise but
anyway

one night
while i was
slopping
the mezcal
down i told
a friend
who told a
friend &
the word
got back
to villa
who after
that wd
grin at me
every time
i passed
him
& then i
knew that
he knew
so the
next time
i was in
texas i
visited the
gun dealer
where the
pistol was
supposed
to be sent
& was
given a
letter sta
ting that
the work

on it
had
been
delayed be
cause the
engraver
was down
w/the
pneumonia
&
that it wd
take another
month or
so before
it cd be
delivered
so
here i
am lost & gone
waddami
gonna tell
villa
i told
my old man
the hard spot
i'd gotten into
& he took
a wooden
pistol down
off a shelf
where he
kept all his
whittled &
handcarved
things &

BOARD

sd don't
rightly
know what
to tell you
i made this
pistol for
tom horn
up in mon
tana & he
liked it so
well he
dug his
initials in
to the bar
rel w/a
little bowie
knife see
right there
T H and
when they
were fix
ing to hang
him he
gave it
back &
don't you
wish this
was the
gun of yr
dreams
i thought
abt it for
a few
seconds
then sd

can i have
it my old
man put a
hand across
his whiskers
& they
scraped on
him some
hate to part
w/it tell you
what i'll
whittle a
nother &
make it
a dead
ringer to
this how
long will
it take
when do
you have
to go back
3 days' time
i'll have
one ready
before you
leave
deal i sd
do you have
any of that
gold paint
left
the next time
i saw villa
i poured him

a drink
& sd
this will
have to do
til i get the
real one
i was wai
ting for
villa to pull
his pistol
& shoot me
out of sheer
frustration
instead
he smiled his
big mustache
smile
put five
hundred bucks
on the table
& sd
amigo
today
i want you
to blow up
one goddam
big train
of all the
witched up
mutherfucken
luck
makley sd
i thought
i was
done for

meat for the
crows
lost
the way
that auto
matic jammed
up on
me
he shoved
a cigaret
into his face
sd
it may as
well have
been made
of wood
wood martin
sd
yeah wood
well here's
a story
that came
down thru
my family
seems
my grampa
got himself
in a fix
up in mon
tana
got his
ass thrown
in jail for
killing a
guy the

sheriff can't
wait for
the hanging
seems
he was
the victim's
best friend
so
he opens
the jail door
a full week
before the
hangman
was due
sez
yr gonna
escape
what's that
grampa sez
yeah
yr gonna
escape &
here's yr
es
cape weapon
a wooden
gun grampa
sez
that's it
that's all
the chance
you get
the sheriff
had no idea
that my

future gram
ma had al
ready smug
gled a gun
to my gram
pa the night
before &
grampa
pulls it outta
his back
pocket &
shoots the
sheriff
gave him
a third eye
whenever
grampa told
the story
he'd pull
out that
wooden
gun &
wave it
around w/
the real one
the best part
was
he'd let
me touch
both guns
for luck
wish i knew
whatever
became of
the wooden

one my
daddy sd
it got burnt
in a house
fire down
in kentucky
& now it's
lost
old man
harnad took
the wooden
pistol out
of his
overall
pocket &
set it down
on the table
even dis
tance between
him &
dillinger
what's this
dillinger sd
a gun
harnad sd
it's not a
real one
i can see
that from
here
it's wooden
i carved
it myself
why
you ever

see one of
yr own
get killed
i don't
have any
children
yr a lucky
man my
boy was
shot down
in front
of the
liberty
national
ten year
ago
next week
what's that
got to do
w/me
everything
nothing
harnad reached
into his
pocket &
pulled out
a city
marshal's star
set it on
the table
you the law
around here
you might say
that
gonna arrest

me
nope
everybody
else might
want you
i don't
what do
you want
dillinger sd
reaching
inside his
coat
i wdn't do
that if i
was you
i got one
man in the
front of
this house
w/a ten
gauge shot
gun
another man
out back
w/a thomp
son sub
machine gun
they're my
other boys
good boys
too if you
know what
i mean
dillinger
relaxed his

hand
that's better
so now what
you stay in
town the night
you paid
for the room
then you leave
just like that
just like that
harnad used his
tongue to
move the
tobacco chew
from his left
cheek to his
right
dillinger smiled
sd you remind
me of some
body harnad
smiled around
his dark teeth
sd i remind
you of no
body then he
got up from
the table
yr forgetting
the wooden
gun
harnad leaned
down close
to dillinger's
face sd

my boy had
that in his
back pocket
when he
got shot
strange no
blood ever
got on it
but i cain't
hardly touch
it w/out
feeling some
kinda sting
it's all lost
now anyways
so i'm giving
it to you
you held up
a bank
w/a wooden
gun
dillinger sd
baby face
grinned &
the darkness
exploded
out of his
face
sure
hell
why not
it was a dare
besides
i had a 45
auto stuck

in my belt
just under
my coat
but when
that cashier
caught sight
of that
wooden gun
she just
abt shit her
pants
blue she
was so
scared &
it wasn't
even that
good of
a carving
had little
cracks &
rough spots
all over
it but i
thought
jesus if i
do this
it'll be the
first time
anybody
pulls a job
w/a wooden
gun i'll go
in the record
books right
along w/the

daltons who
tried to rob
two banks
in one day
i'll be
baby face
paused &
looked
dillinger
in the eyes
& dillinger
sd famous
yeah baby
face sd
but the
daltons got
wiped out
almost to
a man
so what
i had the
wooden gun
in one hand
& a choc
olate bar
in the other
& had to
try it &
i gotta
laugh every
time i think
abt it i
even offered
the cashier
a bit but

she sd
no thank
you
can you
beat that
she sd
no & it
was a per
fectly good
chocolate
bar christ
wd you
of killed
her dillinger
sd
hell i don't
know but
come to
think abt
it i kinda
wanted to
but i didn't
& i don't
know why
except that
she was
scared the
candy tasted
good &
i liked the
look of the
money
all of that
taken to
gether

do you know
what i'm
talking abt
sometimes
when it
gets like
that i try
to leave
everything
alone so
that i can
think abt
it later any
way it took
me off the
killing idea
just long
enough so
i didn't
spooks me
now to
think abt
it you still
got that
wooden
gun
baby face
smiled
sd i gave
it to the
girl right
after she
handed me
the money
& you know

what she
did w/it
she just let
it go out
of her hands
& it came
back across
the counter
& fell on
the floor
& the god
dam barrel
broke right
off snapped
off like a
rotten twig
i really
fucken hated
to see that
because i
kinda liked
that gun &
the girl cda
been my
sister but i
already had
the money
& the girl
was outta
control cry
ing & the
candy
tasted so
jesus christ
good so i

figured i shd
get outta there
while the
getting was
good but i
liked that
girl & i wanted
to shoot her
just to see
her blood &
all & i still
miss that god
dam gun it felt
good in the
hand girls
cdn't have
guns on the
rez billie sd
i knew there
were guns
around but
not for girls
so what i
wd do when
ever we
played guns
was i wd
break a stick
that had a
small branch
growing out
of it you
know snap
it down
shorten it

so you'd
have the
barrel &
the handle
too
nights i'd
put that
stick gun
under my
pillow for
good luck
did it ever
bring you
any
billie grinned
just a no
account bank
robber
the likes
a you
dillinger never
told his
old man
abt the wooden
gun he
found at
the movies
instead
he sneaked
it into
the house
& hid it
under the
bed & when
he had to

turn the lights
off & go
to sleep he'd
put the wooden
gun under
his pillow
dillinger won
dered if a
wooden gun
ever gave
off any light
he tried
talking
to the
wolf but
it wasn't
paying
any atten
tion all it
cd think of
was
meat
& the way
dillinger
knew that
was he
cd see
inside the
wolf's head
he let it
come close
the big
mouth
leaning
open he

was star
ting to
fall in love
w/the
mouth
when he
reached
out & touched
it w/the
barrel of
the wooden
gun the
wolf didn't
seem to
mind the
gun barrel
got a
little
clump of
gray fur
on it
& all
the wolf
did was
smile
just a
little girl
& dillin
ger cdn't
remember
her name
but she
had the
blackest
hair that

dillinger
had ever
seen &
he was al
ways try
ing to
touch it
except for
that one
time when
she brought
dillinger
a present
all wrapped
up in
butcher
paper w/
twine tied
around
it so
tight that
he had
to take
his jack
knife out
to cut
it & even
then the
string wd
grow back
in places
& then he
found out
where the
string was

breathing
there was
a small red
heart
attached to
it & when
he cut that
the string
stopped
breathing
& one
little red
drop came
out on his
hand &
for a second
or 2 it
really stung
like a wasp
had got
him &
then it
was gone
the little
girl w/the
very black
hair was
trying to
tell him
something
he cd see
her lips
moving
but there
wasn't any

sound like
when he
went to
the movies
& the
sound was
off &
somebody
wd have
to get up
& complain
to the pro
jectionist
& the sound
wd come
back on
the sound
had to
come back
on you
cd go
crazy w/
out it
& when
he got the
paper off
he saw
the wooden
gun it
was pain
ted all
black the
barrel was
so black
it left

some of
the night
in his
hand
then the
girl's voice
came back
on again
& she
sd her
father had
made it
she sd
it was
good luck
to touch
& wd
heal any
sores
or wounds
& she
wanted
dillinger
to have it
only when
his skin
touched the
gun barrel
something
funny
happened
not all
of that
part shows
up in the

eyelight
like the
wooden gun
actually
going from
her hand
to his
but the
night lightning
came out
in the air
& stayed
there w/all
the dark
zigzags
going
in all
directions
he liked that
but it
made her
afraid
& she had
to hide
in her hair
then he
was touching
somebody
w/it some
guy in a
uniform &
the man's
clothes
ripped open
the skin

cracking a
part just
under his
rib cage
& dillinger
cd see
inside his
body where
everything
was still
going
heart going
lungs going
blood sur
prised but
still pulsing
thru the
arteries &
veins
at first
this made
dillinger
very afraid
tho he
didn't know
why be
cause this
wasn't
him
who was it
so why
shd he care
but he did
tried putting
the cloth

back to
gether the
way that it
was tried
putting the
skin to
gether
back the
way that
it was
but even
when he
got some
of it pieced it
reminded him
of a jigsaw
puzzle
& when
he cdn't
get the
pieces to
fit just right
he forced
them into
place &
then they
wd pop out
& blood
wd come
out in the
seams &
dillinger wd
try to push
it back like
during a

hog butchering
when he
cupped his
hands to
gether to
catch the
blood
but then
didn't know
where it
was supposed
to go after
that &
touched it
to his lips
the blue
uniform tried
talking
but everything
that it sd
dropped
back
syllable
by syllable
right into
the wound
& that time
a kid got
stabbed w/
a wooden
gun
w/a sharpened
barrel
not supposed
to have the

end sharpened
like
that
the little girl
hiding way
back inside
the black
of her hair
came out
as billie she
sd if i give
you a woo
den gun
will you
promise to
give me
a real one
was crad
ling the
wooden gun
in her arms
like it
was a baby
rocking it
to nighty
night what
happens when
you get the
wooden gun's
shadow on
you makes
you feel so
goddam lost
dillinger isn't
sure this is

the beginning
of a fairy tale
a riddle or
a question
so he just
stayed
quiet while
billie sd
pour a little
cat's blood
on it &
she'll peel
right off
like a
boiled po
tato skin
dillinger
grabbed a
very black
piece of
billie's sha
dow skin
away from
her & ate
it the second
he got it
inside his
mouth it
exploded
all around
his tongue
warm so
warm &
tasted a
little like

licorice
a little like
toe jam
a little like
cum
& then he
was right
in the middle
of robbing
a bank
only he
was all
by himself
he didn't
know what
happened
to red
baby face
or fat charley
they musta
got lost
or the day
wrong &
he was
holding a
thompson
in one hand
& a wooden
gun in the
other
but for
some strange
reason
nobody
was afraid

of the
thompson
it was the
wooden
gun that
had every
one edging
back toward
the wall
some kind
of black
energy was
twisting
off the
wooden
gun &
just hanging
in the
air like
strands of
very dark
smoke
& because
nobody
wanted to
get close
enough to
give dill
inger the
money
thick stacks
of bills
began to
pour out
of the

bank drawers
all by
themselves
& once
they dis
covered where
dillinger was
standing
they headed
toward him
& his
gunny sacks
in thickets
of ravenous
love he
didn't know
how he
got into the
get away
car but
he did
he was
sitting
next to
death
who was
playing
w/some
thing
between
his legs
& driving
& the
roads he
went down

were lost
even
unto
themselves
dillinger
was digging
a grave
along w/a
friend
for his
broken
wooden gun
he'd left it
on some
body's drive
way &
a car tire
had gone
over it
never
heard it
crack
but
somehow
& he
really wasn't
sure how
he cd feel
the car tire
snap
the barrel
off just as
tho the car
had run
over his

arm it
had a dull
snap to it
the crack
going all
the way in
side &
thru him
& when he
& his friend
what name
doesn't
remember
gun or boy
gone boy
& for a
second the
gun had
eyes in the
grip one
on each
side kinda
like a fish
or bird
& they
blinked
out
or
no
how was that
they stuck
open &
when dill
inger tried
to touch them

they went
out like
lights in
a room
wood so
much like
a piece of
his bone
he cd talk
to it the
ground felt
death wet
right at the
rotting point
sd gone
magic when
he placed
the gun in
the ground
& covered
it over by
hand the
guard's face
went
from fear
stupid to
jackass
surprised
when he
saw dill
inger stan
ding in the
half light
w/that
pistol in

his hand
he started
to say some
thing then
dillinger
grabbed
him by
the collar
& spun
him a
round the
fuck
he cd feel
dillinger's
breath
on his
neck yr
the fuck
dillinger
sd jamming
the pistol
barrel into
the guard's
back
do
what i say
you won't
die
somebody
was laugh
ing the
guard sd
you won't
get away
dillinger

sd you
won't live
to see that
asshole
sometimes
dillinger
wd dream
it all
different
or
he wd
dream the
newspaper
version of
the story
w/lots of
stuff he wd
put in
or he wd
rewrite a
totally
different
version
of the story
one where
instead of
the weapon
he'd jammed
into the
guard's back
it was a
thompson
no mis
taking a
machine

gun when
you are the
meat sha
king at the
other end
of the
barrel i
think you
broke my
nose the
guard sd
trying to
shove his
face away
from the
wall the
blood was
starting to
drip out on
the floor they
took out all
the bad
words in
the news
papers but
in his dreams
dillinger
recalls more
than he sd
or less
he wasn't
sure which
but that
was ok
because

nobody wd
get any
of it right
especially
the part
abt the
wooden gun
first theory
he had a
real 45 auto
& a wooden
gun too
second theory
he had just
the 45 auto
& on his
journey up
the corridor
of cells an
inmate slipped
him a wooden
gun he'd just
got done
whittling
third theory
he grabbed a
confiscated
wooden gun
off a guard's
desk on the
way out
& he used
that instead
of the real
45 auto just

to see how
far it wd
get him
sidebar
possibility
g. russell
girardin
in his book
dillinger
edited by
william hel
mer suggests
that herbert
youngblood's
attorney smug
gled a wooden
gun to young
blood & he
slipped the
piece to dill
inger
or maybe it
really was
a 45 auto
everyone
knew that
raoul walsh
was willing
to pay five
thousand dol
lar finder's
fee to the
man or woman
who brought
him dillinger's

wooden gun
no questions
asked
right after
the battle
of the little
bighorn a
lakota warrior
some say
black elk
shoved a
wooden gun
into custer's
hand
this partic
ular wooden
gun had
been stolen
from a rene
gade gun
runner &
was painted
both red &
black for
blood &
death appar
ently black
elk wanted
to give cus
ter a sha
manic clean
sing un
fortunately
several par
ties reached

the battle
scene
before the
burial detail
arrived
& no such
wooden pis
tol was ever
reported
however for
years a red
& black
wooden pis
tol was
displayed
above the
back mirror
in the acme
saloon in
el paso in
fact it was
the last
thing that
wes hardin
saw before
john selman
shot him
in the back
john murrell's
favorite trick
was to hold
up a traveller
on the natchez
trace w/a
wooden pis

tol & when
the victim dis
covered that
murrell was
holding a
wooden gun
wd go for
his only to
be surprised
by a real
pistol that
murrell
pulled out
of his coat
grave marker
carved out of
a fence slat
at the
top a large
wooden gun
hacked out
maybe w/a
hatchet the
whole effect
was to make
the marker
look like a
very gro
tesque cross
dillinger shoved
the thompson
barrel straight
into a guard's
face the
impact of

the muzzle
breaking his
nose & when
he stuck his
hand up to
catch the
blood dill
inger sd make
another move
& i'll blow
yr head off
some of the
blood going
down the
guard's
shirt billy
the kid
had thought
abt using
the wooden
gun that
bob ollinger
kept on his
desk claimed
it was some
thing he'd
won in a
poker game
from doc
holliday &
it had
become his
good luck
charm liked
to hold it

up & say
if i rub this
3 times
kid
that means
yr gonna be
dead
but what
good was
a wooden
gun against
bob's ten
gauge shot
gun
right after
they hanged
texas jack
longman
one of the
vigilantes
stuck a
wooden
gun up the
dead man's
ass some
one sd it
looked odd
like a turd
dead & gone
piquette sd
it wasn't
enough that
dillinger
escaped he
had to rub

people's
noses in
it he had
some guy
carve a
dozen woo
den guns
& then
talked me
into wrap
ping them
up in fancy
packages
& sending
them out
to all kinds
of cops
including
the indiana
prosector
& that lady
sheriff lillian
holley he
even gave
me one
but i'm afraid
to keep it
out where
people will
see it
when i
heard abt
dillinger
escaping jail
w/a wooden

gun i went
up to the
attic & got
out the
old wooden
gun my
grampa
left me
the story
was his grand
father had
it w/him at
kings moun
tain &
he didn't
want santa
ana's boys
to get their
hands on it
so he brought
it w/him in
to the alamo
& when
he was picked
to be one
of the couriers
he asked
travis if he
cd carry that
instead of
a real pistol
since there
was such a
shortage of
arms he'd

rather carry
that old woo
den gun &
his big bowie
knife on his
way out
he surprised
a mexican
sentry by
pointing that
wooden pis
tol at him
& going
bang
every pay
day
which was
the end
of each
month the
boys went
into town
for the ex
press pur
pose of
letting off
some steam
& cree
winslow
who owned
the big
sky gunshop
hated to
see em ride
in because

he knew
that as
soon as
some of
them got
good &
likkered up
they'd start
riding up
& down
the streets
discharging
their pis
tols & the
target they
all aimed
for was
the large
handcarved
wooden
gun that
cree had
hanging
by a big
iron rod
out over
the board
walk in
front of
the shop
he cd
never
rightly ex
plain why
but he loved

BRANCH that big
wooden gun
& hated to
see all the
bullet holes
in it
common
sense told
him that
it wd take
a stick of
dynamite to
destroy this
log of a
gun
or
at the very
least a
couple of
gatling guns
still
every time
that someone
fired a slug
into that
wood it
just abt
killed him
so
this time
he decided
to take matters
into his
own hands
he unlimbered

a pair of
ten gauge
sawed off
shotguns
once carried
by the
sonora kid
& the moment
the cowboys
got themselves
formed up
at the end
of the street
for their
usual charge
thru town
he stepped
outside
holding a
sawed off
in each hand
& walked
out into the
wheel rutted
street to
meet them
the idea hit
him that he
cd very well
be a dead
man w/in
the next few
minutes but
he had al
ready de

cided that
the big
wooden gun
had taken
all the lead
he was going
to allow
the second he
saw them
spur their
horses into
motion he
cocked the
sawed off
hammers
back &
waited
the cowboys
hadn't ex
pected cree
to pull such
a stunt &
when they
got w/in twen
ty feet
they reined
in the foreman
a big irish
man called
shannon o
toole sd
you shd go
inside cree
where you
won't get

shot
cree managed
a nervous
smile
pointed a
sawed off
at shannon
& sd
i can get
you first
the irishman
backed his
horse up
a few steps
& sd you
ain't got the
sand
if any of
yr men fire
on me
or my
wooden gun
i'll kill
you
the irishman
studied the
colt 45 in
his hand
a few moments
laughed
& sd
hell boys
we can't shoot
ole cree
where'll we

go to get
bullets or
have our
guns fixed
lets go
hunting crows
o'toole
waited while
his men
headed back
down
the street
then sd
i got a win
chester w/
a broken
lever
cree sd
leave it
w/me i'll
see what
i can do
hand
nailed to
an oak
tree w/
the index
finger
folded thru
the trigger
guard
of a
wooden gun
the note
nailed be

low it
reads
this is all
that is
left of
bill trego
he sure
did like
this gun
johnnie al
ways kept
the real
wooden
gun for
himself
once
i asked him
if that was
the one
he'd used
to escape
from crown
point just
to see what
he'd say
& he looked
me straight
in the eyes
& i thought
to myself
ok here it
comes be
cause he
cd do that
& not really

tell you
anything
billie he
sez you
know how
it is w/me
they're all
real cuz
i invented
the wooden
gun sure
yeah shit
& i am
the trickster
who made
the missis
sippi river
flow back
wards but
good old
me i went
right along
w/it because
johnnie has
got this
thing this
quality
where even
when he
is lying
you know
some part
of him is
also telling
you the

truth &
pretty soon
he sez
baby
i am the
wooden gun
& i am
the real
gun when
you got me
you got
everything
while he
was in
crown point
i went
to a guy
who makes
anything
wood in
cluding the
best furni
ture anyone
ever laid
eyes on
he does
nothing
but carve
stuff out
of wood
& i had him
make me
a little 25
auto swee
test little

wood pis
tol you
ever laid
eyes on
i almost
love it
more than
the real
one which
i keep in
a crystal
studded hand
bag which
i tell him
is for my
cosmetics
but that
little wooden
25 auto
looks so
real you
can't tell
just by
looking
at it you
have to pick
it up before
you know
that it's
wood i
used it on
a pinkerton
detective
even got his
gun before

he knew
he'd been
had
goddam
he was
pissed
red hamil
ton stubbed
his cigaret
out in his
hand sd
i got this
wooden gun
from a guy
who claimed
it was the
key to a
lost treasure
the thing was
he owed me
ten bucks
& sd it was
the only
thing he had
worth money
so i took it
the treasure
was supposed
to be buried
on a bluff
overlooking
the ohio river
british gold
put there
during the

revolutionary
war so i
took off a
perfectly good
day when
i cd've
been robbing
a bank to
have a look
see for my
self
never found
a goddam
thing except
rusted hatchet
head &
couple of
indian head
pennies
later on when
i was telling
this bootlegger
abt it he
pulls an
identical
wooden gun
out of his
shirt pocket
when we
matched them
together they
cd've been
twins he
smiles pours
me a drink

& sez
looks like
we both've
been had
so bottoms
up lets wash
all the shit
away
big foot
was carrying
a wooden
gun at woun
ded knee
no killing
unless we
have to dill
inger sd
pulling the
bolt back
on the
thompson
youngblood
leaned
close sd
i know how
to kill
people
he had
sweat
running
down his
dark face
big rivers
of it
sd

i sure like
that wooden
gun
dillinger
rammed it
into a guard's
ass the only
thing that
kept it
from going
in farther
than the
cheeks was
trouser cloth
the guard's
mouth went
open like
he was abt
to scream
the cloth was
starting to rip
out at the seam
three days after
dillinger's
crown point
escape gerald
wilson maker
of wooden toys
in davenport
iowa received
one hundred
& four orders
to make wooden
guns just like
john dillinger's

even tho nobody
ever really knew
what dillinger's
gun looked like
most historians
agree that
dillinger's ver
sion was
really a hand
carved barrel
abt four or
five inches
long
& there was
a place at
the back of
the barrel
a slot or
a groove
where some
kind of
wood or
metal grip
cd be fitted
in
but this
has also
been called
mostly
speculation
the only
photograph
of dillinger
holding the
wooden gun

& taken
at his father's
home in
mooresville
indiana
does not
show off
the wooden
gun he is
holding
clearly
one other
snapshot
taken of
dillinger
that day
purportedly
has him
displaying
the wooden
gun for the
camera
the story
has it that
he is holding
it sideways
w/both hands
just barely
grasping the
barrel
so that it
can be
viewed
in all of its
length

but that
photograph
according
to an un
published
biography
which has
subsequently
been lost
that image
no longer
exists
the wooden
gun dillinger
gave his
father
disappeared
shortly
after he
received it
the accepted
theory is
the old man
burned it
in the back
yard
at least one
neighbor
reported
watching
dillinger's
father pour
a whole
can of
kerosene

over some
thing then
igniting
the object &
stepping
back before
tossing a
lit rag on a
stick then
yelling dead
cat
just trying
to get rid
of the
stink
hoffsteader
always
put a
wooden gup
up above
his door
the day
his gang
was going
to make
a cattle
raid no
body ever
suspected
him of
being in
the cattle
rustling
business
but years

STICK

later ronald
north his
official
biographer
verified
the rumor
that for
years hoff
steader had
lead a double
life
as an outlaw
& as a
respected
rancher no
body ever
found out
what happened
to his wooden
gun
pony deal
asked the kid
why he
stole bob
ollinger's
wooden gun
the kid
was indexing
his colt 41
then slowly
sighting along
the barrel
when he sd
bob claimed it
brought him

good luck
so
when you
kill a man
you take all
his luck
he pulled the
wooden gun
out of his
coat &
sd
you figure
this will
bring me
some good
luck pony
it's awful
black kid
makes my
skin itchy
just
to study
on it what
do i think
death sleeps
inside it
makes me
think of scabs
& pus
& blood
on the moon
at apple river
fort we used
to drill w/
snapped off

tree limbs
& big sticks
cuz there
wasn't
enough
rifles to
go around
tho harkle
road the only
one who
got killed
in the battle
hell
he had a
hawken &
used to make
fun of the
stick boys
that's what
he called
us til suther
made him
stop every
body knew
he was a
mountain
man & wd
take
shit from
no one
when har
kleroad
caught that
ball suther
was right

beside him
sd
he was
dead fore
he hit the
ground
suther put
a spanish
doubloon
in the dirt
next to
harkleroad's
body in
case there
was next
a kin
& then
he put this
oak
twig into
the wound
sd
to draw out
the evil
spirits an
old shawnee
trick he'd
learned
back during
the battle
of the thames
sd
you
don't do
this you'll

have demons
playing stick
ball w/his
head & gone
the minute
he took that
twig out
sd you
want it
& i sd
suits me
all the way
up the
river &
into the sky
i made it
into a twig
gun just
tied a strip
a rawhide
around the
y shaped
handle &
was going
to cut the
blood tip
off but
suther sd
doncha dare
that's good
for counten
coup dillin
ger sent
babe ruth
a wooden

gun i know
that for a
fact be
cause i
watched him
write a
little note that
read dear
babe keep
hitting those
home runs
& i'll keep
robbing those
banks &
we'll see
who breaks
the record
first yr all
time friend
john dillinger
he tied the
note on it w/a
little string
& wrapped
the whole
thing in
butcher pa
per i sure
hope the
babe did
not throw
that wooden
gun away
story that
billie fre

chette told
in a bar
i went every
day to see
john dillin
ger not really
to see him
but i went
down to the
jail just to be
there no i didn't
know him
but it felt
like i did
& i kept
looking to
see if his
face was
at a window
i knew it
wdn't be
but you
never know
jesus he
felt like
a brother
to me
i wd talk
to him
at night
when i
went to
bed not
you know
like in

a prayer
but more
like a good
conver
sation &
i wd pre
tend that
he wd
reply like
i knew he
wd & down
around that
jail i lost
count of
all those
guards &
police hol
ding ma
chine guns
never told
nobody this
but i always
took the
toy wooden
gun my
daddy whittled
out of hick
ory for me
it was a nice
shiny well
made little
pistol that
fit right into
the palm
of my hand

& if you
are thinking
as i know
you are
what good
is a wooden
gun against
a machine
gun then
you know
why my
heart is
going so
fast it feels
like it
will jump
right up
my throat
but some
thing in
side me
way back
in the dream
ing place
is telling
me that
the wooden
gun will
keep me
warm &
safe i carry
it
not only
for me but
for dillinger

as well
just before
riding out
of town
the kid
stopped
at ollinger's
corpse
stuck the
wooden
gun barrel
in ollinger's
blood
& tasted
it as tho
it was a
piece of
peppermint
candy
pasted
to a stick
all during
his escape
dillinger
kept think
ing he was
going to
be shot
he cd al
most feel
the bullets
going in
but he
didn't
care he

thought
fuckit
i'm too
close to
getting
out feel
ing the
shock
of the
bullets
& the
soft places
on
billie's skin
every
thing else
blurring
the guards'
faces
going past
like
big smudges
on the
window
of time
only catch
ing a few
of their
words don't
they're
gonna
please
don't i
have kids
dillinger's

teeth showing
between
his lips
things
going out
& coming
back into
focus
youngblood
cd kill
somebody
will have
to watch
him don't
some of
the wall
clocks al
most look
like they've
stopped
some sha
dows along
the floor
appear to
have bled
their
what is it
that builds
up inside
the head
to the blow
ing point
he cd easily
kill machine
gun in his

hand so
heavy &
so murderously
light just
a little
squeeze of
the trigger
you go
that way
for the
keys
if you
shoot me
go for
the legs
but not
the face
or the crotch
ok please
dillinger
at one point
thought he
cd see
bones right
thru the
guard's
skin the
black way
death made
him light up
& then
shoved
him back
under the
blood you

son of a
just around
that corner
don't make
me shoot
you he cd
feel the
heat of the
words
pound in
his throat
&
then what
touched
youngblood
accidentally
w/the thomp
son thought
he saw a
little open
place form
on his arm
where the
wound might
be young
blood sd we
gonna be
famous dill
inger laughed
& sd or
dead you
heard me
move yr ass
against the
wall

now
when we
get out i'm
painting
myself
w/all kindsa
skin
keep yr
mind on
that thomp
son you
ever do a
woman hol
ding a thomp
son dillinger
grinned while
shoving a
guard is
there any
other way
wooden gun
stuck in
the ground
barrel first
the sign of
death by
shooting
wooden gun
stuck in the
ground grip
first barrel
pointing up
the sign of
the outlaw
wooden gun

w/the barrel
snapped off
the sign of
anarchy
oblivion
being so
lost you
will never
get found
the day i
heard they
shot the
montana kid
i tied a
stone to a
wooden gun
& threw
it in the
river it's
called
drowning
the gun
the first
thing that
cagney thought
when he
received
his wooden
gun in the
mail is that
it was some
kind of late
award for
public enemy
then he

saw the
name john
dillinger
when i was
a kid i
used to play
wooden
gun tag
dillinger sd
baby face
sd i had
a cast iron
cap pistol
& a wooden
gun
dillinger sd
when
we used to
play tag
one
kid wanted
the wooden gun
so bad
he was
willing to
trade any
thing for
it yeah baby
face sd like
what he
had this
marbles hun
ting knife
that his
grampa gave

him didja
trade
baby face
asked hell
no dillinger
sd
it was
the best little
handcarved
wooden gun
i ever had
this guy
brought
it back from
the philippine
insurrection
claimed
he'd
killed a guy
for it
didn't
have any kids
&
because he
knew my old
man
& they
got along he
gave it to me
whatever hap
pened to it
baby face
asked the kid
who wanted
it so bad

snapped the
barrel off
did you kill
the little
shithead
baby face
asked
no
i broke his
nose instead
i'da killed
him baby
face sd
cracking
a knuckle
i'da killed
him alright
wooden gun
passed on
to an enemy
is
the initiation
of the feud
code wooden
gun painted
all red
means
gutshot all
black
means
the dreams
are all
turned in
side out lost
wooden gun

w/an all white
barrel is
the sign for
a turd coming
out of death's
asshole
wooden gun
sent to a
fiancee means
if you don't
love me you
will die
alls
i wanted
to do was
scare him
i never figured
he was healed
&
wd shoot
me tanner sd
he held up
his right
hand w/
one finger
missing
& the
worst part of
all was he
got my
fuck finger
now
what am i
gonna do
ross gave

tanner a
long side
ways look
sd
easy
use
yr other
fuck finger
&
don't ever
use a wooden
gun again
after dillinger
got out of
crown point
& returned
to chicago he
looked up
ed wanderly
who
cd carve any
thing out
of wood
& hired him
to make
a wooden
replica of
a thompson
sub machine
gun sd
i want it
w/all move
able parts
it won't shoot
wanderly sd

it'll only
be wood
yeah
i know
dillinger
replied but
i want it
to look so
real it'll
scare the
shit out of
anyone who
isn't touching
it or looking
at it close
up
what's the
point if you
have a real
one wanderly
asked
the point
dillinger sd
handing wan
derly a
hundred dollar
bill is
i want it
to be the
be all &
end all of
not just
machine guns
but of all
guns

anytime
anyhow
anywhere
i want it to
be the finest
looking
wooden
gun ever
made
can you
do it
if you can
escape from
crown point
i can make
you a
machine gun
wanderly sd
a wooden
gun shot all
to pieces
war
a wooden
gun thrown
down a
well nightmare
water &
the black
taste of dream
huckleberry
finn
whittling
a wooden
gun out of
a fence slat

tom sawyer
painting it
the color
of a dead
man's face
annie oakley
shooting
the barrel
off a wooden
gun that
frank butler
held
by the grip
between his
teeth
purvis
smashed
the wooden
gun dill
inger sent
him w/a
hammer
then pul
verized the
slivers
nobody knows
what happened
to billie's wooden
gun but once
she dreamt
that it
went way up
inside her
cunt &
then became

her baby
mathew turner
has conjectured
in his mono
graph the
hero's path
& the shamanic
magic the
riddle of
the wooden
gun that the
escape gun might
indeed
have been
both deadly
firearm
&
an actual
wooden gun
he goes
on to explain
how
billie frechette
cd easily
have approached
a shaman
of her tribe
& had him
bless a wooden
gun & the
magic that
the shaman
endowed the
gun w/might
have doubled

in strength if
billie had
brought the
shaman some
thing personal
of dillinger's
a lock of hair
a piece of
cloth that
had touched
his body
& not been
washed
maybe
one of his
hats &
especially
one of his
firearms a
45 auto wd
have worked
perfectly
once the
wooden gun
had been
blessed &
energized
w/dillinger's
touch the
magic wd
enter the
wooden grain
& sleep
there til
it was in

dillinger's
hands then
all he had
to do was
rub it 3
times &
it wd turn
into a real
pistol cap
able of
firing real
bullets
& once he
no longer
needed it
he cd rub
it 3 times
again &
it wd re
vert back
into a woo
den pistol
& there
wd be no
way to prove
or disprove
that dill
inger had
escaped from
crown point
jail w/a real
pistol
the beauty of it
all was the
myth of the mystery

turner goes
on to explain
that while
the theory
may seem
a bit farfetched
it is not
any more
outrageous
than
say
shrodinger's cat
he continues
by arguing
that if we
even marginally
believe that
maria sabina
cd heal
sick people by
chanting all those
veladas
then it is
again
marginally
possible to
work enough
magic to
change the
atoms of a
wooden gun
into a real
45 automatic
turner calls
this the riddle

of the wooden
gun or
the alchemy
of belief
either you
believe every
thing or
you believe
nothing
eric stamm
counters this
theory in
his short paper
the anarchy
of belief
& the riddle
of the wooden
gun in which
he states
that negative
fractals coupled
w/infinite
mutltiples
make the wooden
gun susceptible
to gross trans
ference how
ever in situations
that stamm
calls the time
shift occult
it is also
quite easy
to believe in
both every

thing &
nothing they
coexist as twins
when dillinger
gave baby
face a
wooden gun
he also
pulled out
a perfect wooden
replica of a
machine gun
& let baby
face touch
the barrel
baby face
stood for a
moment
transfixed
by it all
he both loved
& hated
the little
copy of the
wooden
gun that
dillinger
had used
to escape
from crown
point &
he cdn't
take his
eyes off
the exact

replica of
the thomp
son it was
beyond
beautiful
he touched
the barrel
ran his
fingers a
long it &
felt his
love &
hatred of
dillinger
rising like a
black storm
he both
cd & cdn't
control
the last time
hemingway
saw dashiell
hammett
was at a
hollywood
cocktail party
hemingway
stopped ham
mett in mid
drink & sd
what's the
riddle of
dillinger's
wooden gun
hammett

paused &
sd it's a
mystery no
body knows
anything abt
it for sure
hemingway
gave hammett
a wide mar
tini smile &
sd well yr
the ex pinker
ton man why
don't you
solve it
hammett re
turned hem
ingway's grin
& sd it's
not that kind
of mystery
then what is
it hemingway
sd growing
impatient
hammett
paused again
stared into
his bourbon
& sd the
stuff that
dreams are
made of

Made in the USA